Bruce Rogers, Harriet Manning Whitcomb

Annals and Reminiscences of Jamaica Plain

Bruce Rogers, Harriet Manning Whitcomb

Annals and Reminiscences of Jamaica Plain

ISBN/EAN: 9783337324803

Printed in Europe, USA, Canada, Australia, Japan

Cover: Foto ©ninafisch / pixelio.de

More available books at **www.hansebooks.com**

ANNALS
AND REMINISCENCES
OF
JAMAICA PLAIN

BY

HARRIET MANNING WHITCOMB

CAMBRIDGE

Printed at the Riverside Press

1897

THIS sketch was prepared by request to be read before the Jamaica Plain Ladies' Tuesday Club. Subsequently a desire was expressed to have it put in more permanent form and offered for sale at a Fair for the benefit of the Jamaica Plain Indian Association. Although personally reluctant to appear before the public in this way, I have allowed my desire to aid a good cause and give pleasure to friends who have kindly received my paper to influence me in its publication.

I am indebted to " The Memorial History of Boston," to Drake's "Town of Roxbury," to Dr. Thomas Gray's "Half-Century Sermon," and to the memory of a few of the older residents for some of the dates and incidents given.

If any of these should prove to be inaccurate, I must rely upon the charity and courtesy of my readers for only indulgent criticism.

H. M. W.

ANNALS AND REMINISCENCES OF JAMAICA PLAIN

To collect and review the circumstances and events which have made our homes and those of our ancestors for many generations is more than a pleasant service. We find an interest and fascination in every step of the way, leading us, as it does, into one of the most delightful portions of our country, and introducing us to not a few of the most refined and cultivated, as well as distinguished people of New England.

There is ever a charm about old-fashioned people and places, as about old books and pictures, antique furniture and china; they affect us by the very contrast they afford with ourselves and our surroundings, even though it is with a touch of pathos and sadness.

Long years ago a much traveled man,

who knew our country well, said, "Jamaica
Plain is the Eden of America." He was
not a Bostonian, and our village was still
a part of Roxbury, so that the suggestion
of conceit and boasting over this small
portion of "the Hub" could not be im-
puted to him.

It has often seemed to us that the loving, favoring smile of heaven rested pe-
culiarly upon our plain, environed as it is
by gently rising hills, which, with their
robes of verdure and noble trees, shelter
it from harsh winds, and hold it in the
warmth and freedom of a pure health-
giving atmosphere. Our charming lake,
covering more than sixty-five acres, nestles
like a gem in its western borders, mirror-
ing forms and colors, all of beauty, and
holds upon its banks some of the most
delightful of our homes.

In early days it gave of its clear, soft
waters for the needs of the neighboring
city;[1] while through the eastern portion

[1] The Jamaica Plain Aqueduct Company was incorporated in 1795, and was the first systematic water sys-

of our village the quiet Stony River made glad the farms and yielded power for mill and factory.

We find that the name originally given our village was Pond Plain, but, as early as 1667, it is referred to in an official paper as the " Jamaica End of the Town of Roxbury."

There are differing opinions as to the origin of the present name; some have so far reflected upon our colonial ancestors as to intimate that a decided fondness for Jamaica rum suggested it, and it is doubtless true that the punch bowl had other uses than to be simply ornamental on the sideboards of our grandsires. Others, however, believe that it was given to commemorate Cromwell's acquisition of the island of Jamaica, in 1670, which

tem that the city of Boston had. It extended from the Pond to Fort Hill, and had about forty-five miles of pipes, made of white pine logs, nearly a foot and one half in diameter, with a bore of five and three quarters inches. The average daily supply was about 400,000 gallons. In excavating for the Subway, several specimens of the old wooden pipes have been unearthed in a good state of preservation. — From a recent number of the *Boston Transcript*.

secured to Boston numerous very valuable products.   There seems, to us, to be a peculiar appropriateness to the name, as it signifies in Indian "Isle of Springs," because of the brooks and springs which abounded here, making the land verdant and fertile.   If we cannot to-day boast of grand and stately castles, reared in the olden time, as in the mother country, with guarding moat and bastions, loopholes for crossbows and guns, — silent testimonials of opulence and power, — we yet can bring to view pictures of many a dwelling, gray and brown with weather stains and lichens and folds of ivy, which have held within their walls of oak and cedar people and events whose records thrill our hearts with patriotic pride or affectionate reverence.

In the early times our village was chiefly an agricultural community, and the cultivation of fruits and vegetables for the city supply was the specialty; but here and there were elegant country-seats occupied by government officials, professional and literary men, and city merchants. Some of these homes and people we hope to see, by favoring records and memory's aid, this afternoon.

Until within a short time, near the Boylston Station, stood a very ancient building, with a pitched roof in the rear sloping nearly to the ground, known as the "Curtis Homestead." It is claimed that this was one of the oldest houses in our country, and that, in 1639,[1] William Curtis made a clearing in the forest for it, using the timbers in its construction from his felled trees. The record is that William Curtis married Sarah Eliot, sister of Rev. John Eliot, in Nazing, England, in 1618, and that, in 1632, they came with their four children to Boston, and it is believed that most of those who bear the name of Curtis in our country are direct descendants of this William and Sarah. For about two hundred and fifty years this house was the home of the Curtises, the last occupants being the widow and children of Isaac, seventh in descent from William.

[1] The first dwelling, built in 1633, was a simple log house, and was burned three or four years later.

During the siege of Boston, troops were quartered here and added their record of strife and suffering to that of domestic peace and happiness, in which the "Apostle Eliot" and his estimable wife often shared; and possibly Winthrop, Pynchon, and the Dudleys, and others whose names stand as pioneers of religious liberty in New England.

Emerson has aptly said, "There has never been a clearing made in a forest, that did not let in the light on heroes and heroines."

A few years since, the march of improvement, *so called*, obliterated this genuine relic of colonial days, with the fine old elm, which for more than a century had shaded it and wafted kindly breezes over it.

Although we have no knowledge that the Apostle Eliot ever lived in the "Jamaica End of Roxbury," he is closely identified with our early history and development, and deserves more than a passing notice. In 1689 he gave some seventy-five acres of land, including the tract lying from Orchard to Thomas, and from Centre to Pond streets, " the income from which was to be used for the support of a school and a schoolmaster." The street, hall, and schoolhouse, which bear his name, commemorate his generous gift. This noble man stands out in those early days as a beacon light, shedding an influence for godliness, for education, and for truest philanthropy. Perhaps, in no sphere of his remarkable life does he more command our admiration and reverence than as the friend of the Indian and the negro. His untiring zeal and self-deny-ing labors in their behalf entitle him to be called " the Apostle."

In a letter to a friend in 1659, he writes: " Pity for the poor Indian, and desire to make the name of Christ chief in these dark ends of the earth, and not the rewards of men, were the very first and chief movers in my heart." Nor can we question that these were the all con-trolling motives, when we consider that after acquiring their language, by the aid of a young Pequot, he translated the

entire Bible into their tongue, besides a
psalter, primers, grammars, and other useful books; and all this in addition to
faithfully fulfilling the duties of minister
of the First Church in Roxbury for fifty-
eight years, a record of devotion, diligence,
and scholarship almost unequaled.

One has beautifully summed up his
life in these words:[1] " His missionary zeal
was not less than Saint Paul's, his charity
was as sweet as that of Saint Francis
d'Assisi, and his whole life a testimony
that the call to saintliness has not ceased
and the possibility of it has not died out."
Eliot lived to see the fruits of his devoted
work in the changed character and life
of many of the Indians.   More than two
centuries have elapsed since this leader
in the Indian cause went to his reward,
but his mantle rests to-day on some here
who deeply feel the need and love the
work in behalf of the poor Indian.

In 1663 our Centre Street was laid
out and called the Dedham road or high-

[1] An historical sketch of the First Church in Roxbury,
by Dr. De Normandie.

way, being a direct route from Boston, by way of " the Neck " and Roxbury Street, to Dedham. At that time and for more than one hundred and fifty years after traveling was by horseback, by private carriage, and by the stage-coach. Those who were unable to own horses or pay stage fares walked to and from Boston, often heavily laden.

The accommodation stages would stop for passengers along the route, blowing a horn as they approached the dwelling, wherever a signal had been placed for them. The express stages, used chiefly by business men, running from Providence and the New York boat, took no heavy baggage, required double pay, and made stops only as they needed relays of horses. Four such changes were made from Providence to Boston, and the journey was completed in about four hours. In 1826 the first Jamaica Plain hourlies[1] began to run; the fare was twenty-five cents.

---

[1] One of the old omnibuses was very long, and named Osceola, for an Indian chief, a representation of whom was painted on the side.

They started from Mr. Joshua Seaver's store, and would call for passengers in any part of the village as requested in the order-box.

Mr. Seaver's store, established in 1796, stood on slightly elevated ground farther back from the street than the one now occupied by his grandsons, and connected with his dwelling.

Here, also, was the village post-office for many years, and the favorite meeting-place of the townspeople to discuss local interests, indulge in pleasantries, as well as exchange their coins for fine groceries, small wares, and farming utensils. Our grandparents of that day folded their quarto sheets, sealed, stamped, and addressed them, and paid twelve and one half cents for the privilege of sending them on their mission.[1] The advent of the two-cent postage stamp and the one-cent card was not then dreamed of.

Entering Centre Street at the Railroad

---

[1] At the time to which we refer, postage was regulated by distance. Thus, $6\frac{1}{4}$, $12\frac{1}{2}$, $16\frac{3}{4}$, and even 25 cents, were sometimes necessary.

bridge, frequently confounded with the historic Hog's Bridge,[1] which formerly spanned Stony Brook near Heath Street, we see on the right all that remains of the once extensive and very beautiful estate of the Lowells, a family among the most honored in our State for character, learning, and culture. The original house, built of stone in the latter part of the last century, was modeled from an old castle in Europe, and became the property of Judge John Lowell in 1785, who resided here until his death in 1802. He was President of the Massachusetts Society for promoting agriculture, and his extensive grounds were largely devoted to the cultivation of a variety of the finest fruits and plants. His son, Hon. John Lowell, inherited this estate and the talent and fondness for horticulture and agriculture, and added several fine glass houses, which he filled with rare and beautiful plants, many of them imported from Europe and

---

[1] For the origin of this peculiar name, see the incident which gave rise to it described in Drake's *Town of Roxbury*.

other foreign lands.   He erected the
present commodious mansion.   The aged
lady who has occupied the house until
recently was a sister of Dr. Charles
Lowell, once minister of the West Church,
Boston, and father of Hon. James Russell
Lowell.   The Lowell Institute for free
lectures on scientific, literary, and religious
themes was founded by John Lowell, Jr.

In 1834 the Boston and Providence
Railroad cut through this estate, and from
time to time other innovations have de-
spoiled it of its grandeur and beauty.

We pass several ancient houses, with
associations doubtless dear to the descendants of their first owners, but unknown
to us, and come to Hyde's Square, at the
intersection of Centre, Perkins, and Day
streets.   The triangle in the centre, bordered with shade trees, had a valuable
landmark on it, not a dwelling, but an
old pump, which, if it could voice its
memories, would tell us interesting tales
of weary, dusty travelers, in vehicles, on
horseback, and on foot, of stage-coach
horses, and those of heavy-laden teams

from far away, to which it had given its cooling, refreshing waters, through nearly every day and hour of bygone years.

And now, after a few rods, we come to the well preserved old farmhouse, the Joseph Curtis homestead, built in 1722 by Samuel Curtis, grandson of the first William, for his son Joseph. A descendant with the same name, and fifth in line from William, now resides here, while the broad acres adjoining, bordering the street with graceful elms, smile with the fruits of careful husbandry, and afford ample space for the beautiful homes of four generations of the same family. During the war of the Revolution troops, from Rhode Island, under General Greene, used this house for barracks, the family willingly giving up its space and comforts for their accommodation.

On the corner of Centre and Boylston streets one is attracted by a quaint and picturesque dwelling, in style and setting one of the most interesting of the older houses of our town, which tells the story of its age on one of its chimneys, 1738

being the date. It was erected by Captain
Benjamin Hallowell, who married a Miss
Boylston, of Boston, whose family was
prominent in its early history. He was
a hot-headed, active loyalist, and commis-
sioner of His Majesty's customs, as well
as mandamus councilor, which facts made
him obnoxious to the public, and in 1775,
during the siege of Boston, he found it
wise to hastily vacate his house and seek
refuge in the city. The house was then
appropriated by the patriotic troops for a
hospital, and some of the soldiers who
died were buried in the lot in the rear
of the house. Later the property was
confiscated by the State, and, in 1791,
bought by Dr. Leprilete, who resided here
until his death. He also was buried
in the garden, and a memorial tablet
marked the grave until the remains were
removed to a cemetery. Upon the death
of Captain Hallowell in England, the estate was reclaimed by his widow. His
son, Nicholas Ward, then took his mother's name of Boylston and inherited the
property. Mr. Boylston was a gentleman

of true culture, education, and philanthropy, making valuable donations to
Harvard College, and to several schools.
He is justly honored by having his name
perpetuated not only by our street and
district, but by a bank, market, school,
and street in the city proper. Dr. Benjamin F. Wing purchased this property
in 1845, and it has remained in his family
to the present time.

In 1797, just one hundred years ago,
was erected the stately brick mansion
which, with the ample grounds extending
to the pond, was called " Lakeville." Mr.
Du Ballett first resided here; later it
was the home of Horatio Greenough,
the sculptor, and it is said that he carved
his celebrated group, " The Chanting
Cherubs," while living here. In 1840
Lakeville Place was opened, dividing this
estate, and later made beautiful by the
several residences upon it. Since 1842
the Lakeville mansion has been the home
of Mr. Thomas W. Seaverns and family.
The inception of the Episcopal Church
in our village was largely due to Mr.

Charles Beaumont, father of Mr. Frank Beaumont, who resided in the Lakeville mansion in 1833. The first services were held here, and later in the Village Hall on Thomas Street, Rev. Mr. Howe of St. James Church, Roxbury, officiating. In 1840 a lot of land was purchased of Mr. Charles Beaumont on the site of the present St. John's Street, and a chapel built which was consecrated in 1841 by Bishop Griswold. The rectory was completed in 1849, and " was paid for, in large part, with money raised by the exertions of the Ladies' League." Many of us remember the attractive avenue, bordered with greensward and graceful elms, which led to the little brown church and rectory, the retirement of its situation seeming to be suited to its purpose of worship and quietness. The membership was very small at first, but in a few years it became the church home of some of the most influential people in our town. Rev. E. F. Slafter was the first regularly settled rector, assuming his duties September, 1846. The beautiful stone edifice

erected upon land bequeathed by General
William H. Sumner, son of Governor
Increase Sumner, was ready for the en-
larged church and congregation in 1882.

General Sumner's old residence on the
hill near the present church is beautiful
in situation, and still very attractive.

Near the north corner of Pond Lane
was built, in 1732, a plain, comfortable
house by Benjamin May, great grandson
of Captain John May, one of the earliest
settlers of our village. Captain John
Parker married the daughter of Benjamin
May, and afterwards resided here for
many years, which accounts for its still
holding the name of the "old Parker
house." Here were the high decorated
wooden mantels over large chimney-
places, the paneled wainscoting and ornamented cornices, which adorned many
of the better houses of that period. The
grounds were ample, extending to the
pond, and covered with a variety of fine
fruit and shade trees. Now crowded by
modern buildings into the background,
deprived of its garden, gray with weather

stains, this old house shows few signs of
its birthright.   About the middle of this
century the small cottage still standing
on the lot adjoining the Parker house
was the quiet home of two much esteemed
old ladies, Mrs. Shepard and her daughter Abby.   The mother was then totally
blind, but possessed the sweet content-
ment which not even so great a depriva-
tion and trial could affect.   Miss Abby
devoted the little front room to a store
for small wares, school children's utensils,
and candies, and it was the delight of the
girls and boys to leave their coppers there
in exchange for her good things.

Some of you may recall an episode
connected with this home which might
have had a tragic ending.   Because of
their unprotected condition, and the
drawer in which the small receipts from
the store were kept, an unworthy young
man, belonging to our village, planned
a midnight entrance.   Miss Abby heard
the window raised, and, in her night robe
and cap, faced the intruder, just as he
had entered the room.   She dragged the

surprised and struggling man into the front room, and held him fast, meanwhile calling loudly for help. The aged mother secured a window stick, and dealt unerring blows upon the youth. After a desperate struggle, he escaped, carrying a window frame and many bruises with him, but no money. The neighbors were aroused by Miss Shepard's cries and came to her relief.

We may safely say that not since the war of the Revolution had the midnight silence and peace of our village been disturbed by so exciting an experience. The friends of Miss Shepard presented her with a large, illustrated Bible in appreciation of her courage and bravery.

On the west corner of Pond and Centre streets stands a large mansion house of colonial style, with an air of quiet dignity, in the midst of attractive grounds. In early days it was called " Linden Hall," doubtless because of the magnificent linden-trees which lined the walk to the entrance and shaded the grounds. It was erected in 1755 by John Gould for his son-in-law Rev. John Troutbeck, assistant rector of King's Chapel, where he offici- ated for twenty years.

He was an ardent loyalist and returned to England in 1776. As an example of the change in public sentiment with the lapse of time, we learn that this noted clergyman was a distiller as well, of whom a witty rhymester wrote : —

> " His Sunday aim is to reclaim
>   Those that in vice are sunk.
> When Monday 's come he selleth rum,
>   And gets them plaguey drunk."

This fine estate, extending then in the rear to the pond, was later owned by Mr. Charles W. Greene, a descendant of Gen- eral Nathanael Greene, of revolutionary fame. He enlarged the house by the ad- dition of another story and large wings, and established a successful boarding and day school for lads, fitting many of them for college. Possibly some here may recall that in the school building on the grounds the first Papanti taught some of the parents of the rising generation to dance.

Among the men, since famous, who

graduated from this school, are John Lothrop Motley, the historian, and George William Curtis, the elegant writer and able editor. The scenes and characters in Mr. Curtis's novel " Trumps " were drawn from our village. Dr. Randall, of Roxbury, but recently deceased, who bequeathed $70,000 to Harvard University, was early a student in this school, and also the two brothers of Margaret Fuller, one of whom was afterwards a clergyman and a chaplain in the Union army. Mrs. Greene is referred to in an interesting article recently written by a graduate of the school, as one " for whom no meed of praise could scarcely be excessive, as she was in sober truth a mother to every lad committed to her care."

This property was next purchased by the brothers John and George Williams, who resided here for several years.

On the opposite side of Centre Street, near Green Street, can to-day be seen a two-story cottage, with pointed roofs and dormer windows, which in our day has been known as the Calvin Young house.

This building with its fresh paint and modern style can yet trace its history through a century and a half of years. It was originally owned by Eleazer May, who sold it in 1740 to Benjamin Faneuil, nephew of Peter Faneuil, and in 1760 it became the property of his brother-in-law Benjamin Pemberton.

We may readily believe that Peter Faneuil — the Huguenot who in 1740 erected and gave to the town of Boston the noted hall which bears his name — often shared in the comforts and joys of this home of his niece, Mrs. Susanna Pemberton. About the year 1802, this estate was purchased by Dr. John C. Warren, son of Dr. John Warren, and nephew of General Joseph Warren, hero of Bunker Hill, for a summer residence. He was one of the most distinguished surgeons of our country, and for many years professor of anatomy and surgery at the Harvard Medical School. His name was honored in the recent ether celebration, he having performed the first surgical operation under ether in 1846, and to his

sanction it owed its introduction through-
out America and Europe.

The dwelling was at that time con-
structed after the West Indian style, with
one story and a half front and two in the
rear. An immense chimney buttressed
the north side; a hall extended through
the centre of the house, with doors opening on to piazzas at both ends; the windows in the front rooms extended to the
floor, all conducing to make it an ideal
summer home. The elm, linden, and
horse-chestnut trees near the house were
remarkable for size and symmetry.

Dr. Warren beautified the grounds with
rare plants and shrubs imported from
Europe; they extended over many acres,
including the present Hill, Parley Vale,
Burrage, and Harris estates, and to the
line of the Providence Railroad. Captain
Charles Hill purchased a portion of this
estate about the year 1830, and Mr. Calvin
Young the residence in 1837, when the
radical alterations in the house, which are
apparent to-day, were made.

About the year 1828, the Warren

estate became the property of Samuel G. Goodrich, author of many histories, books of travel, school and story books, the kindly, well-loved Peter Parley of our childhood. What a delight it would be to welcome once more the monthly visit of " Merry's Museum and Parley's Magazine," to read the charming letters to "Billy Bump," the adventures of Gilbert Go Ahead, and puzzle out the charades and enigmas which tested our youthful wits! It was Mr. Goodrich who cut the fine avenue through the ledges and woodland, and erected the ample mansion in the grove, which later, because of financial embarrassment, he transferred to Colonel Fessenden, and ultimately became the property of Mr. Abram French. Then it was that Mr. Goodrich enlarged and improved the building which had been his gardener's cottage, making the quaint and unique house now owned by Mr. George Harris. Here he resided for several years, accomplishing a large amount of literary work, which repaired his fortune, so that on his return from Paris, where he was

United States Ambassador, under President Fillmore, he purchased a country-seat in Jube's Lane, now Forest Hills Street. Mr. Goodrich was in Paris at the time of the abdication of Louis Philippe, was an intimate friend of M. Lamartine, and was of great service through his wise diplomacy. Many of his works were afterwards translated into French by M. du Boisson. While a resident here he was interested in our local affairs, and was genial in his relations with every one. It is related that, on an occasion of a Fourth of July celebration, he gave an after-dinner toast, " To the ladies of Jamaica Plain, not *so very plain either!* "

Here we are tempted to linger for a little longer. We may not be permitted to enter within the precincts of many of the old homes in our town, to view the veritable memorials and relics of early days, but such has been the privilege of some of us in connection with the Harris home. Through many generations of education and culture, treasures in books and music and pictures, in furniture, plate,

and china, have been collected and preserved, until the home has become verily
a museum of rare and beautiful works,
whose possessor is eminently suited to
these delightful surroundings.

Nor can we fail to offer an appreciative
and loving tribute to the two sisters who
have been among our most learned and
accomplished women, and have exempli-
fied through their long lives the quiet
beauty and loveliness of true charity.
The beautiful hill with the adjacent vale,
now occupied by the fine estates of Mrs.
Hook, Mrs. Pratt, and Mr. and Mrs.
Charles F. Sprague, was in the early days
the Harris homestead. Here Dr. Luther
M. Harris, the father, was born. Some
of us remember him as the valued family
physician, who, when burdened with the
infirmities of age, gave up his practice to
Dr. George Faulkner.

One of the most interesting and attractive of the ancestral homes still standing, in this vicinity, is the Greenough
mansion, finely situated on the curve of
Centre and South streets. It has an air

of dignity and spaciousness which many
a more pretentious modern country-seat
fails to match. Although it has been the
home of five generations of the Greenough family, — since about the year
1780, — its history antedates their own-
ership by many years. This estate was
originally of royal dimensions, covering
about one hundred acres, and belonged
to John Polley. In 1752 it was purchased by Commodore Joshua Loring,
one of the Tory gentry, who a few years
later built the present house (1758),
the frame having been brought from England. Commodore Loring was a native
of Roxbury, and did gallant service in
the British navy, in the campaigns against
Canada. He was severely wounded at
the siege of Quebec while in command
on Lake Ontario, and was retired on half
pay when he came to live here. Although probably at heart in sympathy
with those who resisted the injustice of
the English government, for personal
reasons he adhered to the royal cause,
and, on the morning of the battle of Lex-

ington, he left his home and everything belonging to it, and mounting his horse, " with pistol in hand, rode at full speed to Boston." He never returned, but sailing for England soon after settled in High- gate. During the siege of Boston this house was the headquarters of General Greene, and has the honor of having been visited by General George Wash- ington. Colonel David Henley, who had charge of Burgoyne's captive army while at Cambridge, also occupied this house at one time. For a while, it was converted into a hospital for the Roxbury Camp, and some fifty of the soldiers who died here were buried on the grounds, near where the Hillside schoolhouse now stands. The remains have since been removed to the old burial ground on Walter Street. This property also was confiscated, by order of the General Court of April 30, 1779, and was then purchased by Colonel Isaac Sears, a suc- cessful Boston merchant, who had been one of the most active and zealous of the Sons of Liberty, and a member of the Provincial Congress. Soon after (in 1784) it became the property of the first David Stoddard Greenough, son of Thomas Greenough, who had been a member of the Committee of Correspondence in the Revolution.

It was in 1769 that the first church in our village was built, upon land given by Eliot, — on the site of the present stone edifice, — and named the Third Parish, from its relation to the First Parish on Dudley Street and the Second or Upper Parish on Walter Street. And it was to Mrs. Susanna, wife of Benjamin Pemberton, that it owed its origin. The distance from the other churches, and consequent inconvenience of regular attendance, led her to desire a nearer church home. She proposed to her husband, who possessed large means and had no children or near relations, that they should erect a house of worship, principally at their own expense. He heartily engaged in the project, "and in the course of a year the house was completed, with thirty-four square pews, and three long seats for the poor on each side the broad aisle next the pulpit on the ground floor. There were five narrow long pews [for the colored people, several of them slaves] in the front gallery against the wall, and long seats for the singers below."[1]

The Rev. William Gordon, a Scotchman by birth, entered upon his duties as first pastor, July 6, 1772. A few months later Mr. Pemberton conveyed to the parish the house which had been removed from Commodore Loring's estate to the site now occupied by Mrs. Dr. Weld's house, next to the church for a parsonage. It was occupied by Mr. Gordon during the remainder of his pastorate, and by Dr. Thomas Gray, the second pastor, for sixty years.[2] In 1851 the old house was moved to South Street, and later to

[1] Dr. Thomas Gray's *Half-Century Sermon.*

[2] Dr. Thomas Gray was born in Boston, March 16, 1772, and graduated at Harvard College in 1790. He married a daughter of Rev. Samuel Stillman, D. D., pastor of the First Baptist Church in Boston, by whom he was prepared for the ministry, and entered the pastorate at Jamaica Plain, April 22, 1792.

Keyes Street, where it still stands. On account of a disagreement with Dr. Gordon Mr. Pemberton altered his will, in which he had first bequeathed all of his property to this parish " for the support of his future pastors," and left it " in trust for the benefit of the poor of the town of Boston ; " and the income of the fund is still used for this specific purpose. Pemberton Square, once lined with many of the fine residences in Boston, and now the site of our new court-house, honors his name.

The first bell on the old church was presented by Governor John Hancock, in 1783, then a resident here, and bore the inscription, " Thomas Lester, of London, made me, 1742." We can readily appreciate the happiness of the people when first called to their house of worship by the voice of this bell, and can weave threads of joy and of sadness around its echoes. In 1852 this old church was dismantled of its spire and removed to the site of the present Eliot Hall. It was subsequently destroyed by fire. While the stone edifice was being erected the congregation occupied the Baptist Church one half of the Sabbath.

We find Dr. William Gordon a very interesting character of the strict Puritan type. In a word-picture drawn by a friend, we see him when commissioned by Congress to secure Governor Hutchinson's letter-books, "as he ambled on his gentle bay horse, in his short breeches and buckled shoes, his reverend wig and three-cornered hat, worthy the spirit of a native-born patriot." It may not be amiss to add that with all Dr. Gordon's admirable characteristics, his faithful work as a minister, his active interest in the cause of American liberty, his unwavering adherence to his convictions as an opponent to the slave trade, and a champion of the negro, he frequently lacked prudence and good judgment in speech and action. It was because of his severe and public criticism of John Hancock that the governor gave up his summer residence here; it was because of his attack upon the proposed Constitution of Massachusetts, in 1778, that he was summarily dismissed from his office of chaplain in both houses of the Legislature. There is a tradition that the Doctor was somewhat strict and severe in his requirements of the young catechists, and on occasions he resorted to the birch to enforce his teachings. "After punishing several of them one winter day, his feet slipped as he stepped from the icy threshold of the school, and he fell at full length, his hat and wig rolling off his head. Thereupon the boys shouted in high glee, and gave three cheers." The rod gave place to persuasion after that experience.

The little cemetery in the rear of the church was consecrated in 1785. A quiet walk through this "garden of the dead" is full of interest, awakening memories and associations of the past. There are twenty-four tombs and many graves, upon whose ancient, moss-covered headstones we trace familiar names and some unusual epitaphs. The tombs of Dr. Thomas Gray and of the Greenough family, side by side, are particularly noticeable, as, unlike

the others, they have a large bull's-eye of
ground glass inserted in the doors, evi-
dently to admit light into "the chamber of
death." Very few interments have been
made here since the consecration of Forest Hills Cemetery in 1848. Upon the
small triangular lot at the junction of
Centre and South streets the first schoolhouse in our village was erected in 1676.
The land was the gift of John Ruggles,
and John Eliot and Hugh Thomas were
the principal benefactors of the school.
In early days this spot was the muni-
cipal centre of our town; and here, in
1871, was dedicated our beautiful Soldiers'
Monument, in affectionate, grateful re-
membrance of our heroic dead, who gave
their lives in the service of their country
during the Rebellion (1861–65). Eliot
Street was opened to Pond Street in
1800, and at the corner still stands an
old milestone, inscribed: " Five miles to
Boston Town House, 1735. P. Dudley."
The Eliot School was incorporated in
1804, and later, January 17, 1832, the
brick building was dedicated which now

stands on Eliot Street in the centre of
ample grounds.

Within a few months we have witnessed
with feelings of regretful interest the decay and removal of the old house known
to us as the Nathaniel Curtis homestead.
This estate once belonged to Dr. Lemuel
Hayward, a physician of high repute, and
one of the first to practice inoculation for
small-pox in this vicinity. He practiced
medicine here for several years. About
the year 1780, John Hancock, after he re-
signed the presidency of Congress, purchased this place of Dr. Hayward for his
summer residence. He paid for it seven
or eight shares in Long Wharf property,
amounting then in all to about $400, but
at the time of Dr. Hayward's decease,
in 1821, valued at $100,000, — a striking
evidence of growth and financial prosper-
ity in less than fifty years. We learn that
the house was, like many of that period,
one story and a half in height, covering
much space on the ground, and shaded by
fine linden-trees. We love to tarry here
and do grateful honor to this first gov-

ernor of our new State, who, during our
country's struggles for freedom, was one
of the most fearless opposers of British
tyranny, one of the most active of patriots,
and the *first signer* of the Declaration of
Independence.   He was of fine, dignified
presence, six feet in height, with a very
handsome face and gracious manners.   In
public speaking he was eloquent, graceful,
and accomplished, and plainly formed by
nature to act a brilliant part in the affairs
of his time.   According to the customs
of that period with men of fortune, his
apparel was very elaborate and costly, of
velvet and satin, embroidered with gold
and silver lace.   "His equipage was splen-
did, and on public occasions he rode with
six beautiful bay horses and attended by
servants in livery."   Much of his large
fortune was spent for benevolent and useful purposes, Harvard College coming in
for a share.   In the year 1800, Thomas
Hancock, nephew of the governor, built
the house which has recently been destroyed, and resided here until 1819, when
the estate was purchased by Mr. Nathaniel

Curtis, fifth in descent from the first William Curtis. He was a merchant of Boston, highly esteemed, and filled various positions of trust in our town. He resided here during the remainder of his life, a period of thirty-eight years, and died in 1857. He married for his second wife the widow Leeds, who at the time was living in the old Stephen Brewer house, still standing at the end of Thomas Street, and which was afterwards for several years the home of Mr. William D. Ticknor, of the publishing house of Ticknor & Fields. Mrs. Curtis lived in the old house for many years after her husband's death, until we missed the gentle, sweet face, and the kindly, cordial greetings — and the home was desolate.

More than two hundred and fifty years have passed since the first John May, master of a vessel, came from Mayfield, in Sussex, England, and became a resident of Jamaica Plain, and the ancestor of the many who bear the name of May in this country. In 1650 the old house on May's Lane was built by Mr. Bridge, and since

1771 it has been owned and occupied by the direct descendants of John May. It has always been a typical New England fruit farm, noted for the fine quality of its cherries, peaches, pears, apples, and berries of various kinds.   In the early days it covered many acres, including the beautiful hill now occupied by the fine estates of the Bowditch family and others, and the lowlands, extending north and east to Pond and Eliot streets.   During the siege of Boston the house was given up to soldiers for barracks.   Captain Lemuel May was one of the minute-men who responded to the reveille at the break of day on the 19th of April, 1775, and fought valiantly for his country at Lexington and Concord.   This house, of the seventeenth-century pattern, has maintained its original features until very recently, carefully preserved from any sign of neglect or decay.   Possibly a hasty view of the interior of the old homestead will interest us.   Entering by the front porch, we find the small, square entry opens through narrow doorways into low-

studded, irregular shaped rooms, with overhead and corner beams and wain-scoted sides, triangular cupboards and dressers, and convenient little shelves. There are high wooden mantels, adorned with specimens of antique china and brasses over the large bricked fireplaces. In one room an iron crane, with kettles suspended on chains, swings over the fire-dogs piled with logs, and on both sides hang quaint domestic utensils. The narrow stairway, from the little entry, has a halfway landing to economize space, and leads to cosy apartments above, all interesting for their antique furniture and family relics.

And now a glance at the old square barn east of the house, and more pretentious in size than the dwelling, with wide doors opening at both ends, and lofts stacked with fragrant hay. This is the comfortable home of faithful horses and gentle kine, who looked from their stalls and stanchions on the youths and maidens who often made the walls resound with their merriment as they were borne quickly past in the old swing hanging from the creaking rafters.

The well-curb, with its long sweep and old oaken bucket, brings memories, to some of us, of refreshing draughts of pure water, and of delicious cream and butter rolls, which the moss - covered stone shelves far down the well held securely from possible taint. Back of the house ran the babbling brook and emptied into " the ditch," which was often broad and deep enough to merit a more comely name, and was the favorite resort of the young in winter for skating and sledding. But this ancestral home, with all its charms, has passed from view, like many others, leaving but cherished memories.

Captain Charles Brewer, whose fine estate on Pond Street was originally a part of the May farm, was a lineal descendant of Captain John May, on his mother's side. He was born in Boston in 1804, and received his education there, but early developed a fondness for the sea, and for several years was a successful ship-master in the Pacific and East

India trade. In 1836 he established a shipping business in Honolulu, and in 1846 returned with his family to this country, and became a resident of the Plain.[1] Soon after he erected the commodious mansion in the midst of highly cultivated grounds, which was his home during the remainder of his life.

Mr. Edward Bridge was one of the earliest settlers of the town, and it is believed that he built the house, which has recently been taken down by the Park Commission, near the corner of Centre and May streets. The date 1710 was found cut into one of the old timbers, which is still preserved.

Mr. Abijah Seaverns, grandfather of our townsman, resided here with his family for many years. The original Seaverns homestead, owned by Mr. Joel Seaverns, the ancestor of the family, was upon a farm of some fifty-five acres, now included in Forest Hills Cemetery. In this old house, during the later years

---

[1] His mother, Mrs. Abigail May, widow of Moses Brewer, was then living in the old homestead, and died April 24, 1849, aged 80 years.

of Mrs. Abijah Seaverns' life, a small band of the Baptist faith met frequently for religious meetings, and in 1840 took steps to form a church. Soon after they began worship in the Village Hall, and in 1842 the public services of their recognition were held in the Unitarian Church, in which Rev. Dr. Gray then ministered. On October 4, 1843, the new house of worship was dedicated, and on the same day Dr. John O. Choules, an Englishman, was installed as pastor. The little church stood on elevated ground on the east side of Centre Street near Star Lane. On September 26, 1856, this church was destroyed by fire, with its furniture, library, and records. For two years the congregation used the Unitarian house of worship one half of the Sabbath, and the Mather (now Central) Church for evening meetings, accepting the very kind invitations which came from both societies while the fire was still burning. In August, 1859, the present house of worship on the corner of Centre and Myrtle streets was dedicated.

Following May Street to Pond Street, we come to the beautiful estate now owned by Mr. Edward Rice, and formerly by Mr. John J. Low, and here ready fancy rears again the vanished walls of a stately mansion, three stories in height, first occupied by another of the Tory gentry, Sir Francis Bernard, the royal governor of Massachusetts from 1760 to 1769, — the period of our greatest historic interest. The beautiful sloping lawn, shaded with lofty English elms, gave a charming setting to the house, while broad acres, highly cultivated, filled with choice fruit trees, plants, and shrubs, including orange, lemon, fig, cork, and cinnamon trees, and other rare exotics, added grandeur and beauty to the landscape. One can easily call back the old-time scenes within this mansion, of stately official pomp, of social gayety, of dinners and balls, where the dames and maidens were magnificent in brocade and satin and lace, in towering head-gear, and ample panniers; and where the cavaliers rivaled the ladies in their powdered wigs, gorgeous velvet coats and

satin waistcoats, ruffled shirt-fronts and
cuffs, small breeches and silken hose.
We catch a glimpse of them as they troop
through the broad hall (fifty-four feet long
and twenty feet wide), and the wainscoted
tapestried rooms, in the stately minuet or
the livelier contra-dances, and possibly
recognize the forms and faces of Adams,
Hancock, Otis, Warren, and Quincy.
Governor Bernard was an Englishman,
a graduate of Oxford, a man of erudition
and large wealth. He had remarkable
conversational powers, and so tenacious a
memory that he boasted he could repeat
all of Shakespeare's plays. He was a
zealous advocate of the claims of the
Crown, and though professing to sympa-
thize with the men associated with him
in their resistance to unjust taxation, and
other coercive measures of the royal government, he secretly worked against them,
and used his influence to have the British
regiments sent to Boston, and thus ini-
tiated the war. After holding his high
office for nearly ten years, he was recalled
to England, in response to a petition from

the House of Representatives that "he
might be forever removed from the government of the Province." As he de-
parted from Boston the bells were rung,
cannon fired from the wharves, and the
Liberty Tree hung gayly with flags; so
great was the joy of the people to be rid
of him. Lady Bernard did not leave
Jamaica Plain until a year later — in
1770. Sir William Pepperell was the
next resident of this house for about
three years. He was a graduate of Harvard, and, in 1776, became a member of
the Council, and was avowedly in sympathy with the royal cause. During the
siege this house was also occupied by the
patriotic troops, and later used as a hospital. The soldiers who died here were
buried on the hill in the rear of the house.
This property was confiscated in 1779 by
the State, and purchased by Mr. Martin
Brimmer, a Boston merchant, who died
here in 1804. Captain John Prince next
owned it, and took down the old house, a
part of which had stood one hundred and
forty years, and erected the very attract-

ive mansion which has recently given place to the one now occupied by Mr. Rice. Mr. Prince opened the street which bears his name through his estate to Perkins Street, and it has since been the seat of several beautiful residences.

The summer home of Francis Parkman, LL. D., on Prince Street, deserves more than a passing notice, not only because of his great prominence as an historian and writer on scientific horticulture, but for the remarkable beauty of the grounds lying along the shores of the lake and covered with luxuriant and rare shrubs, trees, and plants, many of them models of symmetry and loveliness. One cannot but regret that this homestead has not been preserved in its completeness, as a memorial of this distinguished man.

The old Jonas Chickering estate adjoining Mr. Parkman's, with its lovely water-front, its unique gothic buildings, its vine-covered lodge, and its deer-park, was, in our early days, one of the most charming of our country-seats.

Pinebank, the home of the Perkins

family for nearly a century, with its broad, winding avenue, beneath noble pines and larches, its stately mansion, its many rich landscape features, claimed admiration for its grandeur and nobility.[1]

Returning to South Street, we find that in early days different branches of the Weld family owned and lived upon estates in this portion of our village. The largest and most important of these was the estate which was given to Captain Joseph Weld, by the Province, about the year 1660, in consideration of services rendered. It was bequeathed by him to his son John, and was the home of seven generations of that family, until about the beginning of this century (1806), when it became the property of Mr. Benjamin Bussey. During the Revolutionary War, Weld's Hill was selected by Washington as a rallying point for the patriot army to fall back upon in case of disaster, as it protected the road to Ded-

[1] Perkins Street, known in early days as Connecticut Lane, was named for William Perkins, who came to Roxbury in 1832.

ham, the depot of army supplies. Mr.
Bussey, after a few years, erected the fine
mansion, still standing, and resided here
until his death, in 1842. The late Mr.
Thomas Motley, brother of the historian, was the husband of one of Mr.
Bussey's granddaughters, and occupied
the house with his family until his decease.
This magnificent estate of three hundred
acres was bequeathed to Harvard Uni-
versity for the establishment of a semi-
nary " for instruction in practical agriculture, useful and ornamental gardening,
botany, and such other branches of natural science as may tend to promote a
knowledge of practical agriculture and
the various arts subservient thereto and
connected therewith." The Bussey Institute was built in 1871, and the beautiful Arboretum, embracing one hundred
and sixty acres, has been in process of
development since that time. During
Mr. Bussey's life, and for years after, the
public enjoyed the freedom of these
charming grounds. There were lovely
wood paths, carefully kept, in all direc-

tions. Here was a rustic bridge spanning
the jocund brook; there a willow-bordered
pond, the home of gold and silver fish.
This path wound back and forth to the
summit of Hemlock Mountain, where
was an arbor with seats for resting, sur-
rounded by majestic trees, and where
lovely vistas of the distant hills and nearer
valley could be enjoyed. On the gray
rocks yonder were nature's moss-clad
seats, where one listened to the endless
whispering of the leaves, the prattle of
the happy brook below, and the ever-
changing songs of birds.

" Up springs, at every step, to claim a tear,
  Some little friendship formed in childhood here;
  And not the lightest leaf but trembling teems
  With golden visions and romantic dreams."

Mr. Bussey's life is a remarkable illus-
tration of the success which results from
natural ability and persevering industry.
With very small pecuniary means in early
life, he made the most of every condition
and advantage, and ultimately acquired
large wealth and influence. Possibly
some here may remember the family

coach, with its yellow body and trim-
mings, drawn by four fine horses, in which
Mr. Bussey and his family rode to church
each Sabbath. There is a pleasing tradition that the old gentleman had the
unusual but very gracious habit of bow-
ing to the people near him on all sides
in the church before taking his seat in
his square pew. On the occasion of President Andrew Jackson's visit to Boston,
accompanied by Vice-President Van Bu-
ren, in June, 1833, Mr. Bussey joined the
grand procession in his yellow coach,
drawn by six horses, richly caparisoned,
and attended by liveried servants.

On the opposite side of South Street
one sees the very attractive house known
to us as the Peters homestead, which, in
1799, was built by Captain William Gordon Weld. About three years after making this home, Captain Weld was lost at
sea, leaving his widow, who was a sister of
Judge William Minot, with a large family
of sons and daughters, who have been
very prominent in the interests and development of our town. Mrs. Weld is re-

membered with great respect and admiration for her character and life-work. She
lived to a great age, happy in the pro-
sperity and the loving devotion of her children. We recall the beautiful and touch-
ing scene when her form was carried on
the bier by her noble sons, followed by
the other mourners, all walking from her
house to the family tomb in the little
church cemetery, and lovingly laid at rest,
without the touch of a stranger hand.

Soon after Captain William Weld's
death, the estate was purchased by a Mr.
Wilson, who resided here for a few years.
Mr. Horatio Greenough, the sculptor, also
lived here when young, and it is believed
that he took his first lessons in art of Bi-
non, the French sculptor, in this house.
In 1829 Mr. Edward Peters purchased
it for a summer residence, and it is still
occupied by his descendants. This house
is the finest specimen of the West Indian
style in this vicinity. Stony Brook runs
through the dell back of the garden, with
a line of fine old oaks and butternut-trees
on its banks. Years since, when trench-

ing the land, the smooth bed of the broad Stony River was reached, into which some of the large trees had fallen and lain imbedded in the mud, well preserved. A perfect beaver dam was also discovered there, and marks of beavers' teeth on some of the trees. Various Indian relics have been unearthed in different parts of the place.

About the year 1827, Mr. Stephen M. Weld, son of Captain William G. Weld, established a boarding-school for young men on the site of the present residence of his family, the corner of South and Centre streets, which was very successful during thirty years, pupils coming from many of the States and from Mexico, Cuba, and Yucatan. Weld Hall, connected with Harvard College, was erected by William F. Weld, in memory of his brother Stephen Minot Weld. Dr. Christopher Weld, another son of Captain Weld, was the first homœopathic physician here, and was much esteemed and beloved during his long practice.

Upon the site of the present Seaver

mansion, on Morton Street, near Washington Street, stood the old house, now a few rods further on, the home of the gifted and scholarly Margaret Fuller between the years 1839 and 1842. Her father had died a short time before, and her mother, sister (the late Mrs. Walter Channing), and two brothers made with her the household. In this quiet, rural home, Margaret found time and inspiration for many of her charming outdoor sketches. She often wandered through the lovely walks in Bussey Woods, soft with fallen needles from pine and hemlock, and bright with abundant wild flowers, and drew glowing pictures from nature's wealth which her pen has preserved for us. It was while living here she inaugurated the literary conversations which produced such a marked effect upon the young and old of the women of that time. They were weekly meetings for free conversation on literary and æsthetic topics at which she was the principal talker. They began in the autumn of 1839 at the home of Miss Elizabeth P. Peabody, on

West Street, Boston, and continued through five successive winters. It was also while here that she edited " The Dial," a quarterly journal, in which she was aided by Ralph Waldo Emerson, Theodore Parker, George Ripley, and others. In this old house Ralph Waldo Emerson boarded for a time with a Mrs. Tilden, who afterward had a young ladies' boarding-school at the Cold Spring House on Washington Street, opposite Green Street. In Franklin Park, on Schoolmaster's Hill, may now be seen a bronze tablet, inserted in a boulder, which records the fact that Mr. Emerson lived in a farmhouse on that spot for two years, from 1823 to 1825. The home of Rev. James Freeman Clarke, D. D., on Hillside Avenue, has a lasting interest, because of the noble, beautiful souls who thought and worked there, and gave by spoken and written words strength and counsel and comfort to many.

Returning to Centre Street, we pass south from Eliot Street, and look with interest upon the old Williams house, a

commodious, square building with central
porch and balustrade along the roof-line,
built in 1805 by Stephen Gorham, a Boston merchant. It was for many years the
attractive home of Mr. Moses Williams
and family, and is still in their possession.

The old Hallet, Seaverns, Balch, and
Louder homes, all suggest interesting and
valuable memories, which we would gladly
record did our limits permit. But we are
tempted to spare a few moments for a
stroll through Louder's Lane. Many times
have we proved the truth of Young's
words: " How blessings brighten as they
take their flight! " and they ring in our
hearts to-day as we wander into this picturesque old way; and we love even more
dearly than of yore the quiet, the grassy
sides, the wild growths of roses and black-
berry-bushes, the tangle of ivy and wood-
bine, and the lovely vistas through leafy
framings of sunny hillsides and woods, of
pastures dotted with grazing cattle, and
of peaceful farm homes. It is a country
idyl, sweet and restful! We may slacken
our horse's reins while he crops the way-

side grass, or we may sit on a fallen stone
from the old wall, while we muse of early
days when there was no turnstile to block
our path, but we could wander on around
the loops of Sargent's woods, and gather
at will the blue and white violets, the
anemones and columbines and cowslips,
without a fear of brass-buttoned monitor
or coasting wheelman.

We see again the dignified form of
Manlius Sargent on his stately horse, as
he rode through his wood-roads, and many
another familiar face of those who sought
these rural paths, and cared not yet for
" rapid transit," with its spectral accom-
paniments. And our hope is akin to a
prayer, that what is left of Louder's Lane
may be spared to us yet many years.

The old Winchester house, on the hillside of Centre Street, was built in the
year 1800 by Captain Artemas Winchester, grandfather of the third Artemas, now
residing here, for his young bride, Miss
Anna Fuller, and it was their home
through their long lives.

In early days, whenever a new dwelling
was begun, the neighborhood volunteered

their services, prepared and stoned the cellar and well, often giving days of labor to help on the work. Then at the time of raising the house, as in the case of the Winchester dwelling,— an unusually fine one for the times, — the relatives and friends came from near and far to show their kindly interest and enjoy the tempting and bounteous collation.

This farm originally belonged to Mr. John Morey, who in 1771 presented the clock, which for many years ornamented the front gallery of the First Church, and is to-day faithfully meeting its duties in the Parish House.

Greenbank, a quiet old home overlooking the Arboretum, holds among its treasures a record of a few years, when Rev. William Ware lived there, after resigning his ministry in New York, and wrote those remarkable works, "Zenobia" and "Probus." Mr. Ware was a man of great learning, of classical culture, and elegant accomplishments. His mind was a gallery of pictures which he portrayed in his writings for the profit and delight of others. Dr. Bellows, in his memorial

sermon of Dr. Ware, writes of these books:
"They evinced talents, resources, and
tastes, which could not be traced to any
known writer, while they seemed wholly
beyond the reach of any *unknown* one."

On the corner of Allandale Street and
Centre Street, Peacock Tavern stood a
century ago. It was kept by Captain
Lemuel Child, distinguished for having
led the Minute Company of the Third
Parish in the battle of Lexington. This
tavern was a somewhat noted resort at
that time, being on the direct highway
from Boston to Dedham and Providence,
a stopping-place for travelers and stages
and factory teams. We learn that when
the British officers were in Boston they
frequently made up sleighing and skating
parties, and after exercising on the pond,
came to "The Peacock" for their late
suppers. Doubtless Generals Gage and
Burgoyne indulged in bumpers there, to
help their drooping spirits. The records
state that during the siege of Boston, Generals Washington and Knox and other
distinguished officers were frequent visit-
ors, the former stopping on his way to

New York after the evacuation of Boston.
In May, 1794, Samuel Adams, the grand
old patriot, purchased " The Peacock "
tavern and forty acres of land, and resided
here during his term as governor, and
during the remainder of his life made it
his summer residence.   We are proud to
add this name to our list of honorable
and distinguished men.   It stands insepa-
rably with Washington, Jefferson, Franklin, and Hancock, and they form together
the brightest constellation which illumines
the Revolutionary annals of our country![1]

Some of the most apparent and pleasant indications of growth and progress
in our town have been the establishment,
from time to time, of the churches, which
represent the faith and worship of our
people, the erection of the commodious
school buildings, and the various chari-

[1] Within our recollection, a very small, old house, on
the opposite side of the street, almost hidden from view
by shrubbery and trees, was the humble home of old
Simeon Giles, a negro, who made a precarious living by
wood-chopping and like service for the neighbors.   He
was the son of old Peter, who was a slave of Governor
Adams, valued and kindly treated, and who lived to
number one hundred years.   Long, long ago their tired
bodies were laid at rest in the little graveyard on the hill,

table institutions.   Strongly as we cling
to much that makes the past dear to us,
we rejoice in all that is making this the
golden age of our country.

Within the limits given, it is impossible
to review all of the homes and characters
which have left their impress on our village and made it worthy to be a part of
the admitted " Athens of America."   A
long line of names comes at memory's call,
in the various walks of life, — clergymen,
authors, teachers, physicians, lawyers, and
merchants, men and women whom we
delight to honor.

> " They hurry from out the forgotten past,
>   Through the gathered mist of years,
>   From the halls of memory, dim and vast,
>   Where they have buried lain in the shadows cast
>   By recent joys or fears."

More than three hundred years ago the
poet Drummond wrote : " It is a great
spur to virtue to look back on the worth of
our line.   In this is the memory of the
dead preserved with the living, being more
firm and honorable than an epitaph, and
the living know that band that tieth them
to others."